I0035882

# RAISING

# THE BAR

## Volume 6

Conversations with
Industry Leaders Who Go
*ABOVE & BEYOND*
For Their Customers

FEATURING:

Angela Legh

Dawna Campbell

Melia Diana

Dr. Melissa Balizan, Pharm D

Maggie Bellevue

Maria Koropecky

# Table of Contents

# Opening Hearts Through Stories and Play

You are made of magic. You are MADE of MAGIC! You are made of magic, stardust, and energy. The magic you have inside is love, playfulness, curiosity, and wonder. How often do you access these magical states? It's a sad state of affairs how we forget to choose these mystical states of being.

As adults, we shy away from being playful in public, afraid of being judged. When was the last time you played on a playground structure? Did you only do it because you had young children with you as if they were your ticket to playfulness?

The youngest children display magic in its purest form. As children grow, life, circumstances, and expectations suck the magic out of them. As a result of cultural and social norms, we forget we are magic; we forget that magic happens all around us. Do you want to remember how to have a magical life?

Do you want to live a charmed life? *The Bella Santini Chronicles*, a book series by Angela Legh aimed at 8-11-year old's, reminds children they are made of magic. The readers learn emotional intelligence and tools for navigating through life's difficulties. Each book ends with book club questions designed to open conversations between kids and their parents about some of the challenges children face.

Angela lives a charmed life and seeks to teach others how they can have a magical life, too. Her online course, *You're Kidding Me! Building Blocks to Reclaim Your Wonder*, allows adults to connect to their childlike playfulness, wonder, and curiosity.

Adults who take the course might find themselves dancing in the kitchen, swinging on a child's swing, laughing uproariously, finding ways to add fun to the mundane, and finding wonder and awe in their lives.

# Conversation with Angela Legh

*Your life has been challenging. How is it that you have learned to maintain your sense of playfulness?*

**Angela Legh**: I am an adult child of an alcoholic father; I experienced many adverse early childhood circumstances, including a fire that destroyed our home when I was four. At this tender age, I was farmed out to an unknown family friend for several months. My early childhood led me on a path of undervaluing myself, which ended with a 30+ year marriage to a man whose method of loving me equaled emotional abuse.

All of this culminated in October 2017, when the Tubbs Wildfire destroyed 5000 homes in California's wine country, one of them my family home. Thrown into a tailspin, I was unable to determine who I was. Questions dogged me; am I living the life I want to live? What is it that I need? I had no answers; I was undone.

When the rug was pulled out from under me, all I had left was a relationship that wasn't serving me; I was forced to make hard decisions. For the first time in my life, I chose myself. I decided to find out who I was and who I could be. I left my marriage, then quit my job. I left the wine country. Through these times of trial, I lost my sense of playfulness; at that moment, I didn't know who I was.

*So, what happened? How did you awaken this youthful energy you now have?*

**Angela Legh**: It took me years of personal and spiritual development to re-discover my inner magic. The first year after I left my marriage, I studied forgiveness. I delved into methods of forgiving myself as well as forgiving my ex-husband. I knew this would be a crucial step for me to get out of victimhood if I was going to recapture my sense of wholeness.

In the second year of my healing, I delved into discovering what brought me happiness. I attended events such as Mindvalley A-Fest, an extravaganza of knowledge and entertainment. I learned dancing made me feel free. I realized I could flow in creativity. I discovered freedom from control, whether in a relationship or a work environment, fueled my sense of happiness.

In the third year of my development, I was finally able to tap into my inner magic. I took long walks in the enchanting woods of the Cotswolds in the UK. I stopped and played on the swing set as I walked to and from the grocery store. I discovered the more I allowed my curiosity and wonder to blossom, the happier I was. And the more I let myself play, the more playful I was. I realized I had found and could share tools that could unlock the wonder within— the wonder which restores magic to our lives.

*You talk about reminding children of their inner magic; how do you accomplish this?*

**Angela Legh**: I see myself as a gardener; I plant seeds that can grow into understanding and knowledge. Within the Bella Santini Chronicles books, available on Amazon and Barnes and Noble, seeds are planted to help children achieve calmness and emotional intelligence. Children are reminded of the ease of using their inner magic. Their magic is made of love, wonder, curiosity, and playfulness.

It is through our perceptions we fail to see we have magic. Some of the characters' ideas may challenge the readers' perceptions; they are given an alternative perspective to embrace or let go.

I do the same thing with adults who take my course. I plant seeds. I don't tell the participants what to do; I tell them what worked for me; they are invited to try it. The tools are varied; some tools will work great for one sector of the population; other tools will work great for different sectors. The lenses of perception, forgiveness, curiosity, and wonder are applied through exercises; the participants can use whichever tools work best for them.

As a quantum energy practitioner, I can shift energy and activate an inner sense of wonder and playfulness. Each week of my online course, the participants are given an activation meditation designed to awaken their inner magic.

*Both perception and forgiveness are quoted as components of your inner healing; can you tell us more about how these qualities made a difference in your life?*

**Angela Legh:** I will first speak about perception, specifically my perception of how my ex-husband treated me during our marriage. Right after I left, I saw myself as a victim; all I talked about was what he did to me. I was the innocent party. He was the responsible party. For the first three months, I wanted everyone to know I was the innocent one, the one being mistreated.

One day, I heard myself speaking, and I thought, Do I want to be a person who sounds like that? I said, "No!" I immediately sought ways to change my perceptions. I started delving into forgiveness – if I forgave him, I wouldn't spend time blaming him. I learned about Ho'oponopono, the ancient Huna practice of forgiveness.

I recited the mantra: *Please forgive me, I forgive you, Thank you, I love you,* over and over as I pictured him in my mind. I said it, even though I didn't feel I held any responsibility in our fights. This practice was a significant step in my healing, but it did not change my perspective. I was still the victim.

One day, I was researching more on forgiveness when I ran across a webpage that stripped my perception and whisked me out of the victim mentality. The site discussed soul contracts, a spiritual idea that was new to me. As I read through the commentary, I found understanding… I played a role in our interactions. My part rotated through the archetypal roles of victim, perpetrator, and savior. At times I was his victim; at times, I retaliated, and I was the perpetrator; other times, I acted as a savior, trying to "save him from his pain."

The blog I read helped me understand our souls may choose difficult circumstances for soul growth, and two souls can make a contract before birth, in which they decide to act out a set of circumstances, each choosing a role. When I could rise above my pain and see our lives from a soul perspective, I understood the role he played was as painful as the role I played. This perspective shift was the key to my achievement of complete forgiveness and ticket out of victim mentality.

*Why do you feel that these qualities – magic, wonder, curiosity, and playfulness, are essential in children and adults' lives?*

**Angela Legh**: My research revealed there are myriad benefits associated with each quality. Let's start with playfulness – it just makes life better! There is empirical scientific evidence concerning playfulness in adults, with benefits including enhanced group cohesion, creativity, spontaneity, motivation, positive attitudes, increased productivity, and decreased computer anxiety. For children, play is the primary way they learn both intellectual and social understanding.

Curiosity is another quality that science quotes as an essential component of a happy life. Curiosity drives academic achievement, deepens connections in social interactions, and motivates innovation. Children are innately curious; along with play, their curiosity is what opens their understanding of the world around them. Unfortunately, as discussed by Sir Ken Robinson in his famous Ted talk, schools are killing curiosity. Fortunately, since Sir Ken's speech, there has been a small movement within education to promote curiosity.

Lastly, wonder begets philosophy. An article in Psychology Today states that wonder is a complex emotion involving surprise, curiosity, contemplation, and joy. When you add any of these ingredients into your life, you are adding magic. The more of these you add, the more magical your life will be.

*On LinkedIn, you have written about adding curiosity and playfulness into the work environment. How do these two qualities improve the workplace?*

**Angela Legh**: Curiosity is known to improve achievement, connections, and innovation. In today's business world, innovative companies can pivot to meet changing demands. When an employee uses curiosity to figure a way to create a better widget, the company benefits. Relationships are the lifeblood of sales; anyone who uses curiosity to build connections will be successful.

Playfulness is also beneficial for business. Playfulness amplifies team building, increases motivation, promotes creativity, and increases productivity. If you had a business and offered a magic pill that promised to bring about these results, would you decline the pill? That is assuming there were no terrible side effects.

The bottom line is that any company that embraces playfulness and curiosity as part of its culture is primed to succeed in today's challenging economy. I am creating an executive training seminar (when we can do those again…) where executives can learn to implement a culture of playfulness and curiosity within their company. I believe a play day is fun, but it will not bring lasting results. When a company embraces a culture of playfulness and curiosity, when its employees have the freedom to express joy and creativity, research suggests there is a high probability the company will experience an increase in profits while employee costs shrink.

*How do you implement playfulness, curiosity, and wonder into your life?*

**Angela Legh**: I've found numerous ways to include playfulness in my daily life. My role as a children's' author is highly creative, which brings me much joy. Another role is a gardener, planting seeds of happiness through my online course, which is also very playful. I actively try to add fun to the mundane; when I sweep my kitchen, I may dance to my favorite music. My perspective is also critical–when I see something as a chore, it will not be fun. But when I see the same task as a challenge and an opportunity, I can have fun doing it.

I add playfulness to my day by allowing my inner child out–if I pass by a swing set, I will swing on it. If there is fresh snow on the ground, you might find me making a snow angel. The other morning, I had the strongest desire to jump on my bed, and if I had high ceilings, I would have. I dance when I am in the kitchen. I might serve lunch on a picnic blanket in the living room. I go the extra mile to find a way to make something boring into something fresh and exciting.

I remember a time when my son came home from school. He was frustrated because he couldn't understand the concept behind adding fractions. I decided to show him a way to understand fractions. If I made it fun, he would better absorb the lesson. So, I grabbed a bag of M&M's and poured them on the counter. I had him group them in sets of four, by color. I explained a collection of four equals one set. I had him eat one from a set. Now that set was three-quarters of a set. I had him eat two from another group, turning it into one-half of a set.

I then had him add the two sets from which he ate by grouping them into sets of four. He had a total of five M&Ms between the two sets, which he grouped into one set and one-quarter of a set. We continued to play with the colorful candy until he fully understood how to add fractions. Adding playfulness (plus touch, taste, and color) allowed him to master a complicated mathematical lesson.

I find curiosity helps keep frustration at bay. When I run into a problem, I might say, "Oops. I wonder what it will take to get the result I want?" This approach diffuses the situation and opens me up to examine multiple possibilities. Curiosity also helps me understand my world. Asking questions about how things work, why things do what they do, and how this gets built creates a more profound understanding of my surroundings. I also have an insatiable curiosity to learn all I can about myself, to know myself. This hunger led me on many paths, which resulted in me becoming all I am.

*How can readers find out more about Angela Legh and what's she doing?*

**Angela Legh**: The best place to learn more about me, the programs I offer, my most recent books, or to connect with me is through my website: https://angelalegh.com Input your email address to receive a free complimentary gift! Enjoy!

# About Angela Legh

Angela's mission is to empower children to remember their magic inside and inspire adults to tap into their childlike wonder.

Angela's fairy tale books Empower, Enlighten, and Entertain children. The Bella Santini Chronicles is a series of books featuring a strong female lead character who overcomes adversity through many challenges.

Her online course for adults, You're Kidding Me, promotes the user's childlike wonder within. She shares her love of FUN, teaching others to let go and enjoy life.

Angela's life was filled with adversity, starting as a young child. She has survived an alcoholic parent and escaped from two house fires, as well as a long-term toxic marriage. She seeks to teach children to value themselves so they don't choose into relationships where they are not valued.

**WEBSITE**
AngelaLegh.com

**EMAIL**
angela@angelalegh.com

**LOCATION**
Taos, New Mexico

**FACEBOOK**
Facebook.com/AngelaLeghAuthor

**TWITTER**
bellasantinibo1

**LINKEDIN**
LinkedIn.com/in/Angela-Legh/6b913b184/

# Becoming Financially Fit

There is a reason why award-winning presenter and speaker, Dawna Campbell, is called "The Mind Whisperer" because when people work with Dawna, their lives change! Dawna knows how to get to the subconscious root of the issues keeping people from having the money, relationships, or better health they want. As an energy healer working on the subconscious level, Dawna is all about inspiring others to create an abundant life of happiness, prosperity, and love.

Dawna's passion is empowering purpose-driven and heart-centered people to discover, release, and transform the hidden stuck "why" into prosperity in all areas of your life. Dawna shows you how to do this through her book, "Financially Fit," as a motivational speaker, and in her international private practice. Her primary focus is to reprogram the feelings and emotions that hold them back from a sense of being worthy, true happiness, and internal peace when working with clients. Others take notice when Dawna's clients go through the transformation process.

As a former Financial Advisor, Dawna's expertise is in aligning the energy world of money and finance with the body and mind's energy world to create purposeful health, wealth, and relationships.

Some areas that Dawna can assist:

*Health: Increasing your overall wellness, discreating sickness, and illness

*Wealth: Creating an abundant mindset, manifesting, and increasing prosperity

*Relationships: Attracting more love in your life, soul mates, family, community

*Spiritual: Aligning with your life purpose, path, and direction in life

*Emotional: Releasing trauma and abuse, self-worth, knowing that you matter

Dawna has a Heart-Centered Healing philosophy, bridging together the body and the mind. By leading with the heart on the inside, she creates an abundant mindset full of happiness, prosperity, and love with others.

# Conversation with Dawna Campbell

*What does it mean to be a Mind Whisperer, and how does it help your clients?*

**Dawna Campbell:** The law of attraction says what you think is what attracts back to you. We have over 60,000 thoughts a day that produce a frequency and vibration that send out signals to the universe and other people returning the very energy to us. Most of the time, we are only aware of 10 percent of these thoughts. The remaining 90 percent are hidden in our subconscious, completely unknown to us.

Under the thought is an energy, rather a feeling or emotion, that either blocks the thought from coming into existence or enhances the thought the returning to you. The emotion or feeling gives the thought the fuel to attract back to you magnetically.

As a Mind Whisperer, I have an innate ability to uncover the hidden masked energy behind the thought that is causing the discomfort or pain in someone's life, stopping them from achieving their goals, release it, and transform the energy to create the desired outcome.

This allows the subconscious to send out the correct energy signals to attract back what we desire.

All we did was change the fuel that we gave the thoughts without taking away our attention or focus to what we are consciously aware of.

Clients typically start experiencing more peace, calmness, love, and having a purpose rather than holding onto unresolved anger, sadness, depression, or anxiety that is causing harm to the mental, emotional, and physical health of the person. This is what Mind Whispering is all about, adjusting and changing the energy behind the thoughts to intentionally create a life of happiness, prosperity, and love.

*You have a philosophy of Heart Centered Healing; can you share this philosophy?*

**Dawna Campbell**: The heart is the bridge between the body and mind, spirit, and matter. We discover a life full of joy when the heart is restored, rebalanced, and recreated. The heart is at this very seat of creation. By leading with the true heart, we can create an abundant mindset in our world.

All of life's trials and tribulations leave us with healing our heart space. We don't want to live in depression, loneliness, or anxiety, yet we experience these every day. All of the events we have in life are awakening to a divine love that we came from that formed us. There is always a silver lining and a gift in all situations. We only have to choose to see it.

When the heart receives the healing, it recreates in a new way, bringing in the abundance of energy and life we desire to live. Our heart space is intimate, delicate, and vulnerable. Through the gentleness of releasing old energy that is stuck, we can truly live our best lives.

*How did you transition from being a Financial Advisor to an Energy Healer?*

**Dawna Campbell**: I believe so strongly that everyone deserves a life of abundance and well-being, I choose financial planning as a career. During this time, I was responsible for $500 million of other people's money. My career was incredibly stressful and combined with worry and fear, my body started to break down, and I became incredibly sick.

During the next two years, doctors could not discern the root cause of pain and ill digestion. I turned to natural medicine and healing after maxing out my health insurance without any answers. I learned that I could not digest food, meaning that there was something in my life I was unable to digest. At this pivotal time, as I was regaining my health, my marriage of 14 years ended. I knew that I needed to make different decisions, and the common factor was myself.

I moved to an ashram (spiritual living community) to embody meditation, healing, and learning from the masters. I left the financial services industry only to find myself in an abusive relationship, isolating me from society. Shortly after, I became financially devastated during the global recession following all of the money rules.

When I left the abusive relationship, I made a promise that if my children and I were kept safe, I would dedicate my life to uncovering these universal truths to help others on their healing path. I have devoted my life to learning as much as I could through science, physics, and my natural healing abilities; and realized the emotional impact that we have on ourselves through our thoughts, feelings, and emotions.

*In what three main areas do clients want the greatest transformation?*

**Dawna Campbell**: Clients around the world all want the same things: better health, increased wealth, or enhanced relationships. All three of these areas, health, wealth, and relationships, are interconnected. When you shift in one area, the others also change on a physical, emotional, mental, and spiritual level.

Health is usually the first noticeable area because it relates to our physical body. When we are in a low vibration feeling for an extended period, the emotion will take up residency in the physical body. It will start creating a physical level disease. Each illness and dis-ease has an emotional component tied to it, keeping it charged up with the fuel to keep our body breaking down. The good news is that once the hidden energy is discovered, released, and transformed, the physical body can release the emotion that helped onto and re-create a pathway of health and happiness.

Wealth is another area that is affected. We all desire to have prosperity and abundance in life, but it goes beyond money and wealth. You can have abundance and prosperity in all categories of your life. Money has an intimate part in our lives and affects many of our decisions and choices. Many people allow money to limit what they want, need, or desire.

Relationships are the last category clients usually want to change. Whether it is about attracting a soul mate, working as a couple in a marriage or other relationship, or even in a family environment, we all want to feel love. Love is at the center of our essence and is the most precious of all frequencies that we want to experience. Albert Einstein said it best when he talked about love being the fabric of the universe in a letter to his daughter if only science could open their eyes to see.

*What are the five major emotions that we need to be aware of?*

**Dawna Campbell**: Nikola Tesla said: "*If you want to find the secrets to the universe, think in terms of energy, frequency, and vibration.*" Your emotions and feelings are the vibration and frequency that give your thoughts and feelings energy to propel you forward and return to you what you are asking. However, this is not always a conscious asking since most of the emotions and feelings are in the hidden parts of ourselves.

There are five primary emotions that we have. The feelings that we produce are all subcategories and variations to these five emotions. Usually, a client will start with lower emotions, such as fear, anger, or sadness. They describe the feelings associated with those emotions with what happened in their life. The subconscious mind related to the event with the emotions and feelings creates a 'Mind loop' to repeat a pattern. When the pattern repeats and grows, we recognize it on the surface as ill-health, a relationship ending, or our wealth disappearing.

The top two higher vibrating emotions, happiness, and love are what clients want. These are often the lessons that we are learning, something needed at the time, or the desired outcome. You have the power to change the lower to the higher emotions with a pivot and shift strategy. The five emotions are the surface layer to what is going on underneath. Often, we have to look under the mask to see the hidden pieces in the deep subconscious. The five emotions are fear, anger, sadness, happiness, and love.

*Fear*: There are two types of fear, rational and irrational fear. Rational fear is when you are in danger, and there is a trigger in the survival brain to keep you safe and out of harm's way. An example is catastrophe weather or a car accident. Irrational fear develops when the mind gets stuck thinking it is keeping you safe, but it is doing more harm than good in reality. This type of fear produces different feelings, such as anxiety.

Fear is showing us that love is absent at the moment. As humans, our divine nature is to experience this love, and in the moment of irrational fear, we cannot. Love is hiding in the present moment. If we can shift our perspective, we can understand that the fear's design is to awaken us to love.

*Anger*: Anger is showing us that at the moment, something needs to change. We don't always realize what needs to change, but we know we are not experiencing love on a deep subconscious level.

Anger's design is to wake us up to love. The trick is discovering and finding where the love is at the moment. If we can have the awareness that we are experiencing anger, we have the power to change rather than allow it to go deeper into our minds.

*Sadness*: There are many variations of sadness, such as grief, loss, and loneliness. When we have experienced the loss of a loved one, for example, the body does grieve. The DNA connection is now disconnected. The energy inside you is reaching out to share with another person's life, and the connection isn't there. Sadness is unexpressed love that is held inside of a person, unable to release.

Some sadness is ok but holding onto it permanently as a state of being never resolves the sadness. Holding it inside without a release will create subconscious patterns, keeping you in physical and emotional discord. Sadness needs to express outward to move into the sharing of love with others.

*Happiness*: Happiness is a true expression of love to be shared with others. When joy is present, peace, kindness, and balance are also present. Happiness is on the inside of each one of us, and we share that happiness differently.

One of the fun ways that I help clients is to have them keep a happiness journal. Write daily the times where you felt the most joy and happiness in your life from the day's events. Recording your happy moments will help you keep your focus on happiness and joy, producing contentment and joyful moments.

*Love*: Love is our divine-human nature to experience in life and is measurable with frequency and vibration. Love is formless energy, but yet forms all things. There are many love symbols in a physical form, such as a bouquet of red roses, chocolates at Valentine's, or a gift of jewelry. Other forms of love include a hug or kiss, kind words, or acts of generosity. These all represent the formless energy for us to share in the power of love. The frequency of love heals all things, repairs DNA, and is considered monks' miracle tone.

### What is meant by "money is emotional?"

**Dawna Campbell**: Many clients come wanting to increase their positive cash flow. The hidden energy gets stuck when we use the same words that describe our financial situation and our essence. An example of this is when a client reaches the root of the issue and wants to feel worthy, valued, and appreciated.

These are the same words that describe our financial system, our net worth, how much our assets appreciate, and the value of our accounts.

The universe returns the vibrational frequency of how you feel regardless of the intention around money or yourself. When the hidden energies are discovered, released, and transformed, you become in alignment with creation, and abundance is yours to keep.

Money carries the internal emotions that you feel about yourself. How you think and feel about yourself on the inside is reflected in your money supply. The money will respond differently for each person according to the inside's emotional feelings, allowing money to react emotionally on the outside.

*You mentioned a Pivot and Shift Strategy. How does this work?*

**Dawna Campbell**: Studying with a medicine woman during a critical time in my life taught me a valuable technique. Anytime I was in a situation and did not like the environment, I could "pivot and shift" my body physically. I could stand up, sit down, get a glass of water, or leave the room. Every time you moved, the energy of the room would shift and change.

The medicine woman had us go through a series of exercises through storytelling to apply this technique. We had to think about an event we wanted to change how we felt about it. The activity was to share the story from different viewpoints, such as a comedy, a drama, an angel, a 3rd person observing, and a higher power. The exercise's scope was to teach us to see the different vibrations that existed and select the one that best suits the new story we wanted to create.

I realized that when we felt certain emotions, we could apply the same strategy. In every moment, every possibility of a higher vibrational frequency exists. All we have to do is look at the situation from a different viewpoint. This strategy is the foundation of the art of Mind Whispering. Understand what you experienced and then shift the emotion fueling the thought to a higher frequency to what attracts what you want.

On the subconscious level, what you ask for through the law of attraction materializes as if by magic when you are in this alignment. This transition from the lower to higher feeling is one of the secrets to becoming Financially Fit in all areas of your life, and what I do with my clients daily.

*How can readers find out more about Dawna Campbell and what's she doing?*

**Dawna Campbell**: The best place to connect and learn more about me is on my website: https://dawnacampbell.com.

I would also like to offer a gift, *The 5 Secrets to Becoming Financially Fit*, full of fantastic information: https://financiallyfit.com/free-gift.

You can also interact with me through social media and my business Facebook page, where I have a LIVE show, "Bringing Spirituality into Life." At the end of this chapter, you will have the links to follow me on the different social media platforms. I am excited about seeing you there.

# About Dawna Campbell

Dawna Campbell is known as *The Mind Whisperer*, combining her knowledge, wisdom, and experience to help others create a life of happiness, prosperity, and love.

Dawna has a Bachelor of Business Administration in Finance and Marketing and spent over a decade as a Financial Advisor and Managing Principal for a National Investment Firm. Dawna's passion shifted her back to her childhood gifts of healing. Dawna lived in an Ashram (spiritual living community) for a year to study with mediation masters, learning about the energy body, brain wave patterns, physics, and science.

Dawna is also the author of the #1 Amazon International Best Seller, Financially Fit. Previously, she had a weekly podcast radio show called "Create it Now" on Mind, Body Radio, been featured guest on Business Talk Radio, and Let's Create a Better World with Bobby Elias. She was the visionary behind the global healing movement and is a motivational speaker sharing the stage with David Fagan, Sharon Lechter, Dr. Joe Vitale, and Lisa Nichols. Dawna is featured in over 90 media outlets with an audience of over 85 million readers.

With over 25 years of professional experience, Dawna maintains an international private practice with a heart-centered healing philosophy and shares her techniques through the Financially Fit Program interactive program. She resides in Bigfork, Montana, with her three beautiful children and is the President of her own company, The Healing Heart, Inc.

**WEBSITE**
DawnaCampbell.com

**EMAIL**
contact@dawnacampbell.com

**LOCATION**
Bigfork, Montana

**FACEBOOK**
Facebook.com/DawnaCampbell811

**TWITTER**
Twitter.com/HealingHeartInc

**INSTAGRAM**
Instagram.com/HealingHeartInc

**LINKEDIN**
LinkedIn.com/in/DawnaCampbell

# Relationship Breakthroughs and Breaking Barriers

Melia's mission is to help lost souls find true healing to cultivate fruitful relationships. As an International Best-Selling Author, Award-Winning Contributing Writer, Trainer, Certified Christian Counselor, Podcaster, and Relationship and Dating Coach, she brings forth her God-given spiritual gifts to help others break soul barriers and have the loving relationships they've always desired. She helps Christian women discover their true identity in Christ while embracing the letting go of old behavior patterns, negative mindsets, limiting beliefs, childhood trauma, blocked barriers… and so much more!

Her primary focus is aiding others with the significate importance of having a personal relationship with Jesus Christ. Her heart and passion are to help others dig deeper and detox core wound patterns hindering their relationships. God is the center of her business, as she allows the Holy Spirit to lead and be used as God's vessel; an extension to glorify His Kingdom. This process allows her clients to purge hidden truths, misconceptions, fears, insecurities, and expose those dark and vulnerable areas into the light for an inner healing breakthrough and live a more peaceful life.

Melia's entire career has been devoted to serve and help others prosper. Through her extravagant years in the medical and fitness field, Melia believes people deserve more than fly-by-the-mill or Band-Aid services that don't last. Life lessons take years to understand, develop, comprehend, and deliver properly. With an impact of lasting change, Melia's powerful message and testimony as a faith-based mentor allow everyone to have healthy relationships with others, themselves, and most importantly Jesus Christ.

*"My mission is to help lost souls find true healing to cultivate fruitful relationships. It's my God-given purpose to help others break all barriers and get the inner healing they truly deserve to have loving relationships with others, themselves, and most importantly, Jesus!"*
*– Melia*

# Conversation with Melia Diana

*As a published author, what struggles or obstacles did you overcome to write your books?*

**Melia Diana**: With all that I do to fulfill my calling, the enemy attacks me in every way possible to disrupt God's plans for my life. My new book, "Vertical Relationship: 4 Steps To Salvation & Getting Right With God," was written when I was spiritually, mentally, financially, and emotionally stretched beyond my comfort zone. God asked me to quit my cushy job and follow Him.

I have pushed through financial loss, theft, family emergency visits, and my father almost dying unexpectedly. I was asked to choose God over the most important relationships in my life, even my son, to follow Him. I was tested with a grand gesture. Did I really have faith? Did I choose God over my family and friends? Was I really a Christian woman who loved the Lord with her heart, mind, and soul? It was the most brutal yet transformational year of my life.

*How is your message different from others?*

**Melia Diana**: Everything I do is a spiritual gift from God to glorify His Kingdom and not my own. I prayed and received confirmation from God to fulfill His purpose for my life. With integrity, passion, and sincerity, I'm truly following the Lord's will for my life. Being in the medical and health field for over 14 years has molded, grounded, and shaped me into the woman I am today. I have learned a great deal about relationships by working with others my entire life.

I definitely have expanded my empathy and compassion for hurting souls with an understanding we are all wounded and in need of a Savior. Many people are blinded by their wounds, and it's my calling to be a source of light in the dark for others to witness.

The Lord exposed to me that He has been preparing me my entire life to step into my God-given destiny. Little by little, step by step, He's been prepping me. Every trial I faced helped me to prosper in areas of tremendous growth. We don't always understand God's calling for our lives until we step out of a surface friendship and into a deep kinship with Jesus. We cannot rely upon our own strength, so a personal relationship with Jesus is vital.

*How has your relationship with Jesus changed you?*

**Melia Diana**: I can tell you I was lost and immature before I came to know Jesus as my personal Savior. In the past, I ran to everyone for answers instead of God. I craved and idolized worldly things. I allowed the enemy to keep me in the bondage of sin and had no idea how to rebuke it. I lacked knowledge of the Bible and God's Word that sets us free.

My relationship with Jesus flourished into a beautiful bond. I now hear the gentle whispers of the Holy Spirit. He transformed me into a revitalized woman in Christ. I look forward to spending time with Him daily because this is one way He speaks to His followers. He changed my mind, heart, and soul, and the way I react to and treat people. I no longer carry bitterness or unforgiveness in my heart. My relationship with Jesus changed me forever… Got to love that!

*As a faith-based entrepreneur, what inspired you to write, teach, counsel, and coach people with their relationships?*

**Melia Diana**: With many confirmations, abundant prayer, and hard conversations with Jesus… He called me to use my spiritual gifts to help others. It came to a brutal and honest moment in my life, where I questioned my "genuine purpose" here in the world, which made my spirit content. I wanted to do His will and not my own. I don't take my relationship with Jesus for granted and know it's a gift. My inspiration comes from doing what He's called me to do. When God commands, you listen with an open heart to receive. I didn't want to live my life barely making it through the day or not living it to maximum potential. Otherwise, what's the point? I want to leave a legacy through His calling! I desire to have my books and all materials read... hoping it helps a lost soul in any way possible. Hopefully, years after I have joined God in paradise.

*What's one piece of advice you have when coaching a married or single woman going through a difficult season?*

**Melia Diana**: For the single Christian woman, you will continue to attract the same kind of man in your life if you don't do the necessary inner healing work to be transformed. There are strongholds, weaknesses, and subconscious beliefs we cling to and need to break free of to attract a godly man in your life.

For the married Christian woman, you will have to be vulnerable enough to allow God to step into your marriage. He has to be a part of your marriage if you want it to thrive. You will continue to have the same arguments, want to run, or think that the grass is greener on the other side. Marriage is a lifelong commitment that takes legitimate effort and hard work to prosper.

Regardless, if you are single or married, all women need healing for their soul to get rid of the toxic behavior patterns and have thriving relationships. You have to want to change to break-free of all barriers and have the loving relationship you've always desired. Transformation happens with the help of God because He is our Healer; I'm just His extension. If we don't allow restoration to all areas of an unhealed soul, you will NOT get to the core root of the problems in your relationships.

*What would you tell someone who is scared to do the inner healing transformational work with you?*

**Melia Diana**: For the inner healing to work, you have to dig deep into those hidden and buried wounds for restoration. The cleansing process starts and ends with God. Yes, it's going to hurt, but you have to be vulnerable for this process to succeed.

The one-on-one coaching work I do is transformational and allows my clients to get rid of the toxicity that is destroying their relationships. I would say, stop hiding behind closed doors and suffering. Stop acting like you have it all together on social media. At some point, you will have to say "enough" and want to do something different. Spinning in a hamster wheel is called insanity and does nothing for progression. God wants more of you and your relationships. So, what are you waiting for?

*Why do you think people struggle in their relationships?*

**Melia Diana**: Living in an upside-down world with a fast plethora of choices to make, many are lost and confused with no idea which way is correct and permanent. Jesus said, "I am the way, the truth, and the life. No one can come to the Father except through me" (John 14:16 NLT). So, to have healthy relationships, we must come to His feet to be decontaminated from intoxicating behavior patterns, emotions, and feelings that get us into trouble in the first place.

We struggle as human beings because we are prideful, selfish, and blinded by our painful wounds. We struggle because we hold onto our bitterness, anger, and unforgiveness. We have to go to those hard places if we want lasting fruit. We must learn that we need Jesus and run to Him, not away from Him. He's the only One who can be with you through trials and tribulations of life. Your spouse, boyfriend, pastor, and family will not. I know that seems harsh, but the truth is!

Many put idolatry in front of God and wonder why they still feel lost and incomplete inside their soul. We have unrealistic expectations and misconceptions from people. We believe our way is the only way. We base resolutions off our own experiences. We allow the devil to have a field day with our minds. Most ignore the necessary inner healing they truly need.

We think there is no way out, so we have a pity-party. We believe with negative mindsets and limiting beliefs – we are not worthy. We allow childhood trauma to dictate our future. We allow our past to hold us in bondage of sin. Jesus did not command us to live that way. He wants more for us and our relationships… this is why I'm so passionate about healing and having healthy relationships. A relationship with Jesus is vital, and most people think it's a religion and not a relationship.

We must lean on and trust God for everything in our lives. The world offers temporary illusions of happiness and not permanent solutions for our prolems. Our source is in God alone. The quicker we realize we need Him- we can stop running to idolatry to help fix our brokenness. I learned to run to God for answers to my questions and not the world for them. When we are hurting, we must realize that the world cannot heal broken wounds, but our Father can restore our wounds and hurting souls.

"He heals the brokenhearted and bandages their wounds" (Psalm 147:3 NLT).

*Why is it hard for people to communicate effectively or have healthy romantic relationships?*

**Melia Diana**: Nobody communicates anymore. We run to idolatry and wonder why we have no peace in our hearts. We are easily offended. People run or resist when things get tough. We misconstrue words and have our own interpretations and meanings of others' remarks.

Romantic relationships have been exchanged via text messages. The idea of courting a lady is sending her a wink, thumbs up, or smiley face emoji. Is chivalry dead? Dating apps are taken over by physical stamina, which does not truly fulfill a lifelong commitment. We are driven by lust and temptations thinking they will give us internal happiness.

For our relationships to prosper, we must come to terms with the harsh realization we need something greater than ourselves. We need something that the world cannot give- which is peace for the soul.

"I am leaving you with a gift- peace of mind and heart. And the peace I give is a gift the world cannot give: (John 14:27 NLT).

We must understand that the Bible is the living word of God. It's full of love, truth, and wisdom. Learning to get right with God takes our relationships to a different level. The deeper with delve into

His Word, we can understand the importance of communication and relationships. Therefore, changing our behaviors and the way we communicate with people.

*How can readers find out more about Melia Diana and what's she doing?*

**Melia Diana**: The best way to find out more about me is on my website https://meliadiana.com.

My website offers freebies, magazine articles, videos, signed book copies, and blogs… Get to know more of my heart. If you are tired, fed-up, and truly ready for relational breakthroughs, then book a free "Clarity Call" with me. I will pinpoint the number one reason why you're struggling in your relationships.

Check out my book trailer and reviews of a new uplifting and inspiring non-fiction book, "Vertical Relationship: 4 Steps To Salvation & Getting Right With God." Find out how to enhance your relationship with God. Gain better clarity of your emotions and behavior patterns affecting your relationships. Learn how to defeat complacency of the worldly customs and the enemy's schemes!

The book is available at Amazon.com/dp/B08NT8Y3DH

If you desire to connect with me, follow me on social media, book a clarity call, or join my free Facebook community. You will be uplifted, inspired, and encouraged. My heart is truly dedicated for the Lord and to bring glory to His Kingdom, which is helping others through an inner healing transformation journey to have thriving and loving relationships.

Many will be blessed by your addition, and I can't wait to start helping you! You can find more ways to follow me at the end of this chapter.

# About Melia Diana

Melia Diana is an International Best-Selling Author, Certified Christian Counselor, Award-Winning Contributing Writer, Trainer, Podcaster and Relationship & Dating Coach, specializing in inner healing transformation. Melia's entire career has been solely devoted to serve and help others prosper. She has spent over 14 years in the fitness and medical field as a Certified ACSM Personal Trainer and Licensed Physical Therapist Assistant. She was hand-picked as a Global honoree, and invitation-only selected to be an Executive Contributor for Brainz

Magazine... the 500 Global lists of entrepreneurs and influential leaders for their dedication to helping others. Melia is also a contributing writer for His Favor Christian Magazine.

Melia's heart for God led her to write two powerful faith-based books. International Best-Seller "Overcomer: Redeemed Masterpiece," her chapter is "7 Keys To Finally Have a Godly Man" and her new inspirational book, "Vertical Relationship: 4 Steps To Salvation & Getting Right With God." Both were published during a global pandemic and written to glorify God's Kingdom.

Her extensive certifications and background led her to utilize her faith, knowledge, expertise, spiritual gifts, and personal development to design her Signature Coaching Programs. She developed a unique methodology to help clarify the missing links and identify core root issues hindering God's best.

She takes women through a one-on-one transformational healing journey, guided by the Holy Spirit, for the restoration of their hurting souls. She helps women discover their true identity in Christ while embracing the letting go of toxic wound patterns. With a godly approach, she helps women to break all barriers and have loving relationships they've always desired.

Melia's empathetic approach encourages others for growth, wisdom, and a stronger mindset. As God is part of her business, she allows the Holy Spirit to guide every woman and man that crosses her path.

**WEBSITE**
MeliaDiana.com

**EMAIL**
info@meliadiana.com

**LOCATION**
Deerfield Beach, Florida

**FACEBOOK**
Facebook.com/TheVerticalRelationshipShow

**INSTAGRAM**
Instagram.com/VerticalRelationship

**PINTEREST**
Pinterest.com/VerticalRelationship/_created/

**YOUTUBE**
YouTube.com/channel/UCvRvQc5lJGI_p3iReyrlE7g

**LINKEDIN**
LinkedIn.com/in/MeliaDiana/

**PODCAST**
Podcasts.apple.com/us/podcast/vertical-relationship-show-faith-based-relationship/id1558700757

# Health & Medicine
# The Amazing Journey

Dr. Melissa Balizan's life's purpose is to save lives. She empowers women to take charge of their health and their life. When working with her clients, her whole health approach includes looking at the root cause, helping them to focus on simple things that can be changed.

She walks alongside these women on their health journey educating, supporting, guiding, motivating, and encouraging. She helps them find their sense of self-love, self-worth, and self-empowerment. Dr. Melissa is passionate about health and patient care, reducing chronic conditions and the healthcare burden. She uses speaking engagements to further educate on women's health.

Dr. Melissa has poured herself into being a servant leader, knowing there is a solution to any problem, assisting her clients in finding the right solution for them, whether that be eastern or western medicine.

As Zig Ziglar said, "You can get everything in life you want if you will just help enough other people get what they want"

She works with women searching for a better solution, a holistic approach, and those searching for ways to be healthier or stay healthy. She helps these women find their voice and lets them know they have a choice when it comes to their health. That is why she is so passionate about educating, especially unbiased education, guiding where necessary, and nudging when warranted so that her clients can make informed decisions about their health.

She wakes up each morning with a grateful heart and desire to help others become the best versions of themselves.

# Conversation with
# Dr. Melissa Balizan, Pharm D

*What inspired you to pursue a career in pharmacy?*

**Dr. Melissa Balizan**: I was inspired to pursue a career in pharmacy because I loved science and math and wanted to be involved in helping others. My mom has a rare blood disease, and I wanted to find a cure for her and thought pharmacy would be a good start. When I looked into pharmacy, I realized there were many directions I could pursue other than just filling prescriptions.

I wanted to be able to help people and encourage them. Pharmacy opened many doors, and I found I was not stuck in a cubical day in and day out. I could still make a difference and help people by having a consulting business to help others reduce chronic disease and educate my clients. I am committed to helping others and make a difference in their lives.

*How did you get into the consulting/concierge side of pharmacy?*

**Dr. Melissa Balizan**: I met several people who would come to my clinics and ask questions. Also, at the institution I used to work for, I was a resource to patients, clients, and physicians, educating them on supplementation that might be available and favorable with the current medications they were taking. I could look at the medications, supplements, vitamins, and herbals a client was taking and streamline a plan to optimize their health and improve their quality of life with the minimum number of medications and supplements, allowing them to have the best and healthiest life ever!

As a concierge pharmacist, I take the time to care for my patients and medical practitioners by providing a comprehensive review of medications, supplements, and health history. Then, I can make recommendations to them to achieve definite outcomes that improve their quality of life.

### Who is your ideal client?

**Dr. Melissa Balizan**: I focus my attention on women in their 40s and 50s who are juggling very busy jobs and still maintaining home life and raising children. I want them to know they have a choice in managing the stress that goes along with this lifestyle. Some are executives and small business owners who take very little time for themselves. I want them to realize the need for self-care.

I use a holistic approach to help women improve their overall health. I want them to find joy in their life and set goals that will help their relationships and balance their lives.

The perfect prospect to work with is a woman in her 40s to 50s. She is in the middle of her career and most likely feels tapped out. She's giving her all to her job and feels she's neglecting herself and her family. She's been pushed to the limit and feels like she's been taken advantage of. She doesn't want to be the 'bad guy' and complain, but she needs time for herself. She needs to feel loved and wanted. She may pamper herself from time to time, but it isn't enough.

I'm looking for those who need a little guidance but are afraid to ask for help. They continue to live life with stress nearly killing them. It could be a heart attack, panic attack, or stroke. They are looking for better choices but not sure who to ask. They've tried eating healthy and may have been doing the right things, but stress can kill.

There is something missing, and they feel it. They need to do something now before a major medical issue crops up. They need to take action and learn self-love, self-care, and stress management. Self-care includes taking good care of yourself, your mind, body, and spirit. It could be exercise, nourishing food, prayer, rest, and sleep.

*What do you mean by holistic approach?*

**Dr. Melissa Balizan**: You must look at the whole body. The mind, spirit, and body all play important parts of our life's health. Nutrition and body movement play a role as well. You need to look at the whole picture and not try to fix one little problem and expect great benefits. Get to the root of the problem. Using the holistic approach opens a new world where you can see changes happening.

I educate and assist women in gaining awareness of their health needs and starting a plan of action. It won't happen overnight; it takes time to make changes and adapt to healthier habits. I will guide them through their journey and give them informative tips for what might work even if they have tried and failed before.

*Why would women need you?*

**Dr. Melissa Balizan**: Many women have tried it all, and they want a better, healthier life. They need someone like me to walk beside them and encourage them to a better healthier way of life. I can help make sense of why something might not be appropriate for them as it might interact with their current medications or supplements. A supplement stating all-natural does not mean it is necessarily safe when there are lots of supplements out there. There are great ones and several not-so-great ones on the market; getting a good quality supplement is essential.

Think about going to the physician's office because you're not feeling well. Often, it's a form of stress that brought you there. A headache, back pain, or a number of other things could cause sluggishness and low energy. Physicians can give you what you need to fix the immediate problem like cream for a rash, or a pill for anxiety, or breathing exercises.

When you have lab work done and a physician tells you that you need to take a blood pressure medication, high cholesterol medication, and you're borderline diabetic. If you do not watch what you are consuming then you're going to take additional medications.

Your doctor tells you to watch your diet, exercise, and fill your prescriptions. You don't know what questions to ask the pharmacist and you're thinking *I should have asked the physician more questions.*

This is where consulting with me comes in. I can guide you on your journey to better health. I can look at your labs and see what medications you are taking and determine if those are the most appropriate. I will work with your physician to give you options based on your health goals. I also review what supplements you are taking and look at your overall health to see what is best for you.

I have the education and experience to give you informed information so you can make the right decision. I will be there to walk alongside you on your health journey to encourage and support your decisions, answer your questions, and help guide you through the challenging time ahead.

Being able to introduce simple steps to empower you to live a healthy life and show self-love. Simple steps include drinking more water, exercising, get that nutrition plan going, and take five minutes for yourself. You will see you look and feel better and have more energy to do the things you want to do, like sharing and spending time with family and friends.

### What is self-love?

**Dr. Melissa Balizan:** How many of us can say we experience self-love? Is it as simple as just loving yourself? The Bible says love thy neighbor as thyself and to treat your body as a temple. So, what does that really mean? Is it taking good care of yourself? If you are treating yourself well, then you can treat your neighbor as you're treating yourself.

If you take five minutes in the shower to meditate and want to improve yourself, then take time to pamper yourself. Take a bubble bath, pray, start journaling, gratitude practices, exercise, take a walk remembering that you need to love yourself.

One of the greatest love stories is the love you have for yourself. The more you love yourself, the more your Cup will overflow, and you will be able to give so much more to others.

### Why do you say people have a choice?

**Dr. Melissa Balizan**: We all make choices every day, so why not choose to be healthy? We have the choice to decide what is best for our health. Helping you realize there may be other solutions or avenues than the normal standard of care. We have to take a leap of faith now and then. Putting yourself first is usually hard to do but we need to love ourselves, another choice.

I had to make a choice in my career, and I decided to use my education to help others attain their health goals. I plan to be there to help and support you in your choices. Everything happens for a reason. You may not realize it until later. It took me four years to realize the stress of my job was causing physical damage to my body. I let boundaries slide and did not maintain myself. I have been there, and I can help you through the process of gaining a healthier you.

*How did you become so passionate about your career?*

**Dr. Melissa Balizan**: I've seen what eastern and western medicine can be and have worked in the health care system and have seen the good and the bad. I am motivated by wanting to help others. Family has been an encouragement to me. As a young girl, my mom drew a staircase and told me to take one step at a time because I might fall if I try to take more. Everything we tackle, every little nugget, we will see the golden result when we get to the finish line. I want to be able to help 25,000 women in the next year reach their health goals. My goal is to help decrease chronic disease by combining eastern and western medicine and will be a guide on your health care journey.

Having the knowledge to help the love of my life. My husband came home from the hospital a slave to pills four times a day. I had to watch him suffer side effects from these drugs. He was unable to live a normal life, but we changed that. I can look at your history and help you also. Cancer, anxiety, depression, and stomach aches are some of the stressors that can cause heart attacks and strokes. Don't just talk about getting healthy. Reach out to me and let me help you achieve your goals. We live in such a fast-paced world with more electronics than you can count, and we don't realize how much they induce stress in our lives.

*What are the next steps for people who want more information?*

**Dr. Melissa Balizan**: You can reach me at my website DrMelissaBalizan.com or on inktr.ee/drmelissab.

*What does my amazing health journey look like?*

**Dr. Melissa Balizan**: Zig Ziglar said, "Motivation gets you going, and habit gets you there." Habits are important because they dictate the results of your life. Habits do not happen overnight. We learn habits from our parents, teachers, preachers, and friends. You must be consistent with them as they take time to develop. I practice prayer, gratitude, meditation, walking, and reading a good book.

You should look at your mindset and stay alert and fresh on your spiritual journey. Pay attention to your physical well-being, keep moving, and pay attention to how you handle stress. How are you handling your stress right now? Do you tip the bottle of pills just to get through your day? Do you feel sluggish and not yourself?

Connect with me.

# About Dr. Melissa Balizan, Pharm D

Dr. Melissa Balizan is the Founder and CEO of Colorado Wife Consulting. She has a passion for health and working with clients who are looking for better choices.

As an author and speaker, she educates on women's health, self-care, and stress management, showing you have a voice and a choice when it comes to your health.

As a consultant and concierge pharmacist, she serves as an advocate for your health and medicine needs with 21 years of healthcare experience combing eastern and western medicine. Her focus is serving others by empowering them to optimize their health.

Dr. Melissa looks at the whole picture of health; physical, mental, and spiritual, while walking alongside you on your health journey. The primary focus is on making a difference in your life one simple step at a time so that you can have a better quality of life.

Dr. Melissa is an expert in women's health, stress management, anxiety reduction, depression, and pain management. She uses her pharmaceutical training and knowledge of medications, supplements, nutrition, physical and mental health as she guides you on your health journey.

She empowers women to make informed health decisions, allowing them to have a voice and a choice. The reduction of the prevalent and chronic conditions has enhanced the life span of many of her clients.

**WEBSITE**
DRMelissaBalizan.com

**EMAIL**
doc@drmelissabalizan.com

**LOCATION**
Online

## FACEBOOK
Facebook.com/Melissa.Balizan
Facebook.com/DRMelissaBalizan

## TWITTER
Twitter.com/BalizanMelissa

## INSTAGRAM
Instagram.com/DRMelissaBalizan

## LINKEDIN
LinkedIn.com/in/DRMelissaBalizan

# The Apostle of Purpose

The befitting epithet that aptly describes Maggie Bellevue is 'Apostle of Purpose.' Fondly and popularly known as 'Pastor Maggie,' she is a Christian minister, international speaker, women's advocate, and transformational leader. Employing the platform of her Kingdom Empowerment International Ministries, she has creatively deployed her vocation as a minister to spiritually empower people and help them identify their life's purpose and propel them towards manifesting that purpose. Pastor Maggie's pre-eminent preoccupation as an 'Apostle of Purpose' becomes evident in the tools she is employing to fulfill her mission.

In recent years, she has emerged as a major force for transformation in the lives of many through personal development seminars uniquely designed to help them identify their life's purpose and to live in that purpose. Additionally, she has authored two books on the subject of 'Purpose,' principally to provide a solid intellectual and theological platform that will power the vision for her ministry work over the next ten years. To add an audiovisual component to that vision, she has only recently established a YouTube channel called 'The Apostle of Purpose.'

Pastor Maggie authoritatively teaches that purpose gives meaning to our existence by offering us the sense of direction that guides our behavior and paths in alignment with our goals and objectives. She teaches that we need to live with a mission that both fuels our motivation and gives our life meaning in such a way that we are inspired to make a significant contribution to the world. Pastor Maggie declares that the greatest miracle in life is the discovery of true purpose. The second greatest miracle is the faithful pursuit of that purpose, for with it comes true happiness, wealth, and fulfillment.

# Conversation with Maggie Bellevue

*You seem to have gradually gained a pedigree as an 'Apostle of Purpose.' To you, what does the word 'purpose' actually connote?*

**Maggie Bellevue**: The word 'purpose' exists within two contextual meanings. The dictionary broadly defines it as the reason why something exists; an intended end, aim, or goal. It also has a connotation in which it is contextually defined in terms of one's life or activities. Accordingly, one might refer to one's actions as being carried out in a purposeful manner.

A life lived with purpose is a life lived with meaning. That means purpose is what gives meaning to our existence by offering us a sense of direction, guiding our behavior and paths in alignment with our goals and objectives. That is why any reference to discovering purpose in one's life is actually asking one to discover the real meaning for one's existence.

As Socrates, the Greek philosopher, once put it, "The unexamined life is not worth living." Success is the progressive realization of worthy goals. Yet, to seek success of any sort, whether vocational or material, purely for its own sake and nothing else, can ultimately render one's life empty, if not altogether meaningless. That is why it is important to seek a greater meaning or purpose to our existence and its attendant struggles. Expressed differently, we need to live with a sense of purpose in which we dedicate our lives to a cause that is beyond us. Naturally, it also means living with a mission that fuels our motivation and gives our life meaning and direction so that we are inspired to make a significant contribution to the world.

*What is the philosophical backing for the need to discover our life purpose?*

**Maggie Bellevue**: Purpose gives meaning to one's life, and, more often than not, it is a lack of meaning in their lives that drives most people to want to conform to others and seek those fleeting and ineffectual pleasures that inevitably prove to be a hindrance to living a life of fulfillment. For most people, it is only after the baffling and protracted feelings of meaninglessness that seem to accompany their so-called successes that they finally ask themselves questions like, "What is the real purpose of my existence?" "Why am I here?" "What am I meant to do while here?" and "Who am I meant to be, and what am I meant to do?"

The two most important days of one's life are the day one was born and the day one finds out why one was born. Yet, the attempt to discover the purpose for one's existence is never an easy quest. It requires genuine commitment. It requires effort. Most of all, it requires a certain curiosity borne of the knowledge that one's sojourn on Earth must have some deeper meaning beyond an everyday mundane existence. Ultimately, however, the greatest miracle in one's life is discovering the true purpose for one's existence.

The second greatest miracle is the faithful pursuit of that purpose, for with it comes true happiness, wealth, and fulfillment. We can view our life purpose a 'guiding light,' and we simply cannot thrive until we discover that light. There is stunning beauty in discovering this guiding light. It gives us a joy that shines brighter, from one day to the next, as we encounter challenges and situations that reveal more and more about our purpose. In the final analysis, the only thing that can guarantee authentic and sustainable happiness in life is the faithful pursuit of purpose. All else is ineffectual commentary.

*Why is it of such compelling necessity to discover our true life purpose?*

**Maggie Bellevue:** There are five reasons why we need to have and live a life of purpose. The first step in our quest to live our most conscious life ought to be discovering of our life purpose. We may well be busy with a million tasks every day yet be headed in no effectual direction if we don't have a clear purpose. That is simply because our goals may not be in alignment with our purpose. Expressed in graphic terms, as we ascend the ladder of life, it becomes imperative that we ensure that it is leaning against the right wall. Clearly, it would be unfortunate for us to pursue our current goals for the next twenty years only to become disenchanted with our final outcome and realize that this wasn't what we wanted after all.

Secondly, we develop clarity on what is important and what is unimportant. Most of us are perennially caught up in activities that ultimately make little or no difference to the pursuit of our worthy goals. Purpose allows us to immediately see which goals are important and which are not. Only when we discover our purpose can we direct our focus to the really important things.

Thirdly, we will start to live a life of meaning. It is only when we pursue our purpose that our life assumes both meaningful direction and authentic meaning. Instead of wasting time on a job we don't love, we can now start working towards a career that better fits our purpose. Instead of remaining exposed to toxic people who are totally incompatible with our purpose and goals, we can now seek out those people who genuinely share those same values that can build our highest life.

Fourthly, pursuit of purpose will give us an unbelievable burst of energy that will sustain our worthy efforts at actualization. The opportunity to pursue our life purpose will fill us with so much energy that each day simply becomes a cauldron of steaming passion for us. Each morning, we would leap out of bed, excited at what we will achieve that day. At night, one might actually dread going to sleep simply because one would much rather be living one's purpose than dissipating eight hours into sleep!

On the obverse, those who are robbed of the wonderful opportunity to live their purpose barely endure each day. Even as they look forward to the temporary respite that the weekend affords them from the dreary weekdays, they start the vicious cycle all over again on Mondays with agonizing resistance.

Finally, we will start to see, and achieve success purely on our own terms. Expressed in simpler terms, rather than see success as an end in itself, it might serve our purpose better to first identify what we truly care about, and then direct our energy into making that our ultimate reality. That is why purpose is so important. When we discover our true purpose, we will naturally want to devote our lives to pursuing it since it is also the source of our greatest sense of fulfillment. Naturally, we want to spend time doing it because we sincerely care about it, and we will get better at it since we are effortlessly prepared to deploy to it all the time necessary to cultivate the experience and skills we need to succeed in it.

*What enduring rewards might we reap from discovering our purpose in life?*

**Maggie Bellevue:** Let us take it from first principles. The fundamental reason why many of us go through life toiling on seemingly difficult, unproductive, and stressful life ventures is that we have not taken out time to discover our purpose in life. The rewards of taking the time to find our purpose far outweigh any professional and financial benefits that may accrue from studying at the best schools and getting the highest paid jobs.

Without seeking and finding our purpose, all those seeming dividends of success will merely ring hollow at the end of the day. We have heard of many people who end up depressed and unfulfilled after working tirelessly for an entire lifetime in a field that ended up being at variance with a true purpose they never took the time to discover. Admittedly, some people seem to be lucky enough to find their purpose at an early age, either by accident or serendipitously. However, for the vast majority, this is not the case.

We need to deliberately devote time to digging deep for those treasures of the soul that come wrapped as the beautiful package called our purpose. We need to intentionally calm down and subject our life to a thorough examination instead of spending an entire lifetime jumping from one unfulfilling venture to the next searching for what makes us truly happy. Ultimately, the greatest reward in finding our true life purpose is genuine happiness and contentment.

*In what areas do we actually connect with our life purpose, and genuinely express it?*

**Maggie Bellevue**: The first thing to acknowledge is that purpose is unique to one, and there are three main areas through which one typically connects with and expresses a purposeful life. The first area is a career or vocation that is meaningfully aligned with our personal values. The second area lies in aligning our relationship to family, friends, and community with our personal values, while the third is the attempt to seek meaning and fulfillment through our spiritual beliefs. In a nutshell, the three areas are vocation, social, and spiritual.

Some people align with their purpose in just one of these areas, while others align with their purpose in more than one. What is of overarching importance is to know one's purpose, and to live one's life in pursuit of it. Living with purpose also means working, connecting with, and understanding one's purpose so well that one can consciously choose to align with that purpose in one of more areas of their life as I previously described.

Closely allied to our purpose are our values, and that is why we need to identify our core values in each area of life, including our spiritual wellbeing, work, family, and friends. To live with purpose is to live with intention. Living intentionally means we have a plan for where we are going, and so we intentionally allow our values to guide us as we make choices and set goals for our lives.

*At what critical point do we acknowledge the Divine nature of the quest for our life purpose?*

**Maggie Bellevue:** Finding our life purpose is a divine exercise. It cannot be otherwise since that purpose resides inside each one of us, typically not something we consciously choose or something someone else can offer us as a gift. Purpose is something we have to coax to emerge from deep within ourselves through self-exploration. Purpose is not unlike a treasure that we have to dig deep to unearth. To discover purpose is to activate God's plan for our lives on earth. God's image is imprinted on our purpose. That means both the image of God, and our purpose, lie within us. Essentially, God hid our purpose, locking it within us. However, He also ensured that the resources we need to unearth that purpose are available within us.

Each of us carries a divine DNA. No one's DNA is identical to another's. In essence, each one of us carries a unique DNA that is coded by God in such a manner as to help unlock certain spiritual dimensions so that purpose can be birthed. Our DNA is truly singularly unique.

For instance, our eyes possess certain characteristics that can unlock our cell phones simply by recognizing those characteristics. Our fingerprints can open doors and elevators by virtue of their uniqueness. This means our DNA creates a unique ID that gives us access to any facility we can possibly imagine. Ultimately, therefore, we are created with invisible and secret codes that can serve as the key to tremendous transformational change in our environment.

*Why do most people go through life without living their true and authentic lives of purpose?*

**Maggie Bellevue**: Four obstacles stand in our way. The first obstacle is the result of faulty programming in our early, formative years. We are tragically programmed from childhood to believe that what resonates within us as a genuine inner yearning is either a total impossibility or is not the right course for us, so we become conditioned into an inauthentic reality. We become so emotionally and psychically paralyzed that we no longer recognize the huge potential that lies like a slumbering giant within us. We blissfully and ignorantly approach adulthood with this faulty mindset, and as our years on Earth accumulate, so do the layers of fear, insecurity, and prejudice to subsume the jewels that are our natural passions, similarly to how layers of sand accumulate to submerge the precious rubies on the beach due to the ocean's tidal waves.

Ultimately, our life purpose becomes so buried in our soul as to become not even remotely recognizable, and until our mortal forms become residents of the graveyard, with our unwritten and unsung music still inside us. That is the reason why the graveyard is sometimes sardonically said to be the richest place on Earth. Indeed, the graveyard is the richest repository of tragically unfulfilled human potential and raw genius.

The second obstacle is that the love we have for those close to us can be so misplaced and misguided that we forget to love ourselves. We tend to shy away from hurting those who have the responsibility for guiding us in our early, formative years. We are in tune with our deeper yearnings, but we are loathe to offend those around us, and we choose to pursue the dreams they have for us to the detriment of our own dreams. The tragic outcome of this tendency is that we end up leading the lives that such people prescribe for us. We have to rid ourselves of the limiting beliefs imposed upon us by our so-called loved ones.

The third obstacle is that most of us exist in mortal fear of failure. Yet, God is actually committed to helping us achieve our worthy goals, as long as they are pursued with love, purpose, passion, and a total submission to His Will.

The fourth obstacle, totally incredulous as it may seem, is the deep-seated fear of the success and fulfillment we seek, which is why most of us self-sabotage ourselves. That explains why, most of us, just when the rewards of a life of honest and fervent toil are within our reach, proceed to commit a series of stupid errors and never attain our desired goals.

*You have authored two books on the subject of 'Purpose.' Tell us about these books. What are they supposed to achieve in the overall vision for your own purpose?*

**Maggie Bellevue:** The first book is, "TREASURES OF THE SOUL - Unearthing God's Purpose For Your Life." My divine assignment was to write a book that broadly discusses 'purpose' in a focused a manner. The book is presented in a unique format called The 7 Cs of Living In Purpose; the 7 Cs being, Conceive, Confidence, Concentrate, Consistence, Commitment, Character and Celebration, and it provides the framework for living life, and living it more abundantly.

The format ultimately provides an integrated and logical system by which the book can be totally life transforming. Its overall message is that there is a living well deep inside of each one of us, and from which a river of living water flows into all aspects of our life. As we dig deeper, we will discover this treasure of our own soul. As soon as we discover this treasure, we have also discovered our purpose here on Earth, and by the same token, the precise reason for our creation.

The second book, "THE PURPOSE DEVOTIONAL - Biblical Illustrations of Those Who Lived In God's Purpose," was motivated by a desire to create a daily reference book that would not only be a logical follow up to my earlier work, "Treasures of The Soul - Unearthing God's Purpose For Your Life," but also one that would possess genuine utility by using

God's people in the Old and New Testaments of the Bible to illustrate how He deploys His divine Will to achieve

His ultimate purpose in the life of each one of us. All the characters featured in the devotional, whether hero or villain, were called by God to do something that was merely a part of His overall purpose, both in the life of the individual, and for the unfolding destiny of Mankind. The book is both a devotional and a companion, being a handbook of action techniques for purposeful living.

The book can be useful in three ways. One; it can be read whole, as one would any other book. Two; it fundamentally serves as a devotional. Three; If one has a problem, randomly opening the book after praying and mediating on the problem might lead one to the page that can offer sufficient insight and direction for confronting the problem. Naturally, this is spiritual guidance based on the fact that the text is fundamentally derived from the Word of God.

*How can readers find out more about Maggie Bellevue and what she's doing?*

**Maggie Bellevue**: The best place to learn more about me and connect with me is on my website: www.Maggiebellevue.com

You can connect with me to be educated, entertained, and delighted on

Facebook: Facebook.com/Maggiebellevue

Twitter: @MaggieBellevue

I would be sincerely delighted to connect with you on these platforms. I can't wait to see you.

# About Maggie Bellevue

Maggie Bellevue is a Christian minister, women's advocate, international speaker, and transformational leader. For the past eighteen years, she has traveled throughout Europe, Africa, America, Canada, and the Caribbean, sharing God's word through her Kingdom Empowerment International Ministries. She also provides socio-economic empowerment of disenfranchised communities and marginalized populations, and advocates for the rights of women and children.

In recent years, she has emerged as a major force for transformation in the lives of many through personal development seminars uniquely designed to spiritually empower people and help them identify their life's purpose, propelling them towards manifesting that purpose. To provide a solid intellectual, literary, and theological platform for her mission as an 'Apostle of Purpose,' she has authored two books, "TREASURES OF THE SOUL - Unearthing God's Purpose For Your Life," and "THE PURPOSE DEVOTIONAL - Biblical Illustrations of Those Who Lived In God's Purpose."

**WEBSITE**
Maggiebellevue.com

**EMAIL**
Bellevuemaggie@gmail.com

**LOCATION**
The Apostle of Purpose, 6632 Bustleton Ave, Philadelphia, PA 19149

**FACEBOOK**
Facebook.com/MaggieBellevue

**TWITTER**
@MaggieBellevue

**INSTAGRAM**
Instagram.com/MaggieBellevue

## LINKEDIN
LinkedIn.com/in/Maggie-Bellevue-a7ba43119

## YOUTUBE
YouTube.com/channel/UCRFKXzidn5Zj0cqLn0nkA3w

## Spiritual Wellness Coach and Author

Maria Koropecky's work is all about sparking inspiration in her clients using methods that they may not have thought of themselves. As a woman with a deep connection to the world around her, she draws on the earth's power and the age-old crystals formed there to uplift and motivate the people she works with. But her work doesn't stop at well-being. Knowing just how much of a problem writer's block can be for budding novelists, she wants to give them a toolkit to write the stories they were born to tell and do so from the heart.

She has written a novel based on her own life experiences and knows just how freeing an experience it can be. So, she helps her clients to tap into the energy of crystals, chakras, and colours, encouraging them to find their voice and share their gifts as she does. Maria understands that success is always just around the corner. You just have to find a way to your keep creativity flowing long enough to find it.

# Conversation with Maria Koropecky

*How did you find your purpose? What led you to this point?*

**Maria Koropecky:** When I think about my purpose, I picture a lighthouse standing tall on theedge of a rocky cliff, lighting the way for ships sailing by during a stormy night. That's what Iaim to do with my business: I try to help people find their way to their goals, no matter how stormy the circumstances may be. I remember visiting the red and white lighthouseat Peggy's Cove in Nova Scotia when I was a kid and the impression that left on me. But it wasn't until the onset of the COVID-19 Pandemic in 2020 that I realized I needed to shine my own light – now more than ever – and help the people I meet navigate their ships during these uncertain times and come out stronger on the other side.

*How did it feel when you started sharing your Crystal Mapping idea with others?*

**Maria Koropecky:** It felt fantastic, like I'd made a real breakthrough in my business – andnot just for myself, but for my clients, too. I'm excited about

Crystal Mapping. It's a coaching tool I created that helps people figure out exactly where they are now and where they would like to go next using the wisdom of crystals. Once I started sharing my crystal map with others, I realized that the crystals my clients picked, based on their own intuition from a selection of 44 choices, were actually a tangible metaphor of their spiritual path.

*I saw online that you had helped your clients feel inspired to write their own books. What was your process?*

**Maria Koropecky:** In September of 2019, when I was 50, I went on a solo backpacking trip across Spain and walked the last 263 kilometers of the Camino Frances. And, as luck would have it, the idea for my forthcoming book *Who Is Donna Tiva?* came to me during my travels. While I was there, I decided to channel everything I had learned during my trip into an uplifting narrative. And now that the first book is ready for publication, I am in the process of working on two sequels. Together, they will form a trilogy, all of which started from that one trip to Spain!

When I told people about my adventure and how it inspired me to write my novel, they started looking at their own lives with fresh eyes and felt motivated to begin writing life-changing stories, too. By working with me, they came to realize that if they had a story to tell, there was noreason why they shouldn't tell it. If I can do it, they can, too.

*How can the readers get a similar result? What would be the steps they need to take?*

**Maria Koropecky:** If someone wants to write a novel based on their own life experiences, I recommend following these four simple steps:

1. Write in a journal every day. You never know what ideas will hit you when you put pen to paper! Plus, keeping a journal gets you in the habit of writing regularly.

2. Read for pleasure, and hopefully, the different stories and the range of narrative voices will spark inspiration.

3. Interact with other writers. You can help to motivate one another and guide each other through the journey of writing a book.

4. Spend time in nature and allow yourself to take in the beauty of the world around you.

These activities will help to keep the river of creativity flowing.

*What has most surprised you about your journey so far?*

**Maria Koropecky:** I have been most surprised and delighted by how many people worldwide like rocks, crystals and gemstones, and, like me, have their own collections. There are also many people who are curious about crystals and what they can do for you, whether they know anything about them yet or not.

When I talk to people about crystals, some women admit that they keep a Rose Quartz in their bra, which can help to balance the emotions, bring about feelings of peace and calm, and support emotional healing. Others have told me that they keep an Amethyst under their pillow for good dreams.

And I've found that you just never know when you might come across someone with an interest in crystals! One of my actress friends once told me about how she bumped into an old friend at the grocery store, and the next thing they knew, they went for a coffee and were emptying their purses, showing each other which crystals they carried with them wherever they went.

*What mistakes did you make and how could you have avoided them?*

**Maria Koropecky:** As an introvert myself, I've been laying low and playing small for far too long. But, had I known that connecting with the natural world and meeting new people would make me feel more alive, I would have gone out into the world sooner.

The earth, in particular, has come to be an excellent source of energy and power for me in recent years. Placing my hands on trees during my wellness walks helps me feel connected to the earth. If I'm not able to go outside, sometimes I like to hold a Tree Agate crystal in my hands. It represents anything with a network of branches, like lightning, snowflakes, and even neuropathways in the brain! It can also represent things like banks and railroad tracks, but it is especially emblematic of trees. However, this is something that I only started doing later on in my life. Who knows what I could have achieved had I known earlier on?

Either way, I don't feel as alone as I used to these days, and I am constantly reminded that we are all connected.

*What have people's reactions been like towards you? What are the highlights and how did you deal with any negative reactions?*

**Maria Koropecky**: Sometimes, people think that talking about crystals is a bit woo-woo. As a result, people out there haven't really taken me or what I do very seriously. But, for all of the sceptics that are brazen enough to say something about it, I simply remind them that holding a crystal is like holding the universe in their hand and that there is actually some science involved, which a lot of people either forget or just don't know in the first place.

For example, did you know that crystals are millions of years old and that their energy comes from deep within the earth? When I tell people that, their guard usually starts to come down. Soon they relax and smile. It really is wonderful to witness.

I have also found that many people tell me they don't know anything about crystals but sign up for a Crystal Mapping session with me anyway. When I give a reading, I may focus on the color of the crystal my client picks, the shape, the mineral content, the folklore, my intuitive hunches, and/or the crystal's name, depending on what I think the client needs. One woman chose the Pink Botswana Agate, and when I said that it's also called the "Sunset Stone," like a romantic walk along the beach, she said at first: "I don't know about that!" But, later, she told me it was spot on

*What challenges have you faced and how did you overcome them?*

**Maria Koropecky:** Being a single woman in a relationship culture has definitely been one of my biggest challenges. I was often made to feel like there was something wrong with me, simply because I wasn't married and raising kids. Being single has allowed me to work on myself and my writing, too, and create cool stuff like Crystal Mapping sessions, which may not have happened if I was focused on other things. I'm learning to accept myself as I am and the path that I have chosen. And, if a wonderful relationshipcomes along or it doesn't, I still know I have a lot to offer.

*How do you plan on further growing your business?*

**Maria Koropecky**: I'm offering free, monthly workshops, including Overcome Writers Blocks With Gifts From Mother Nature online workshops, Crystal Mapping sessions, and a Write From Your Heart coaching program. In 2022, if circumstances permit, I would like to offer writing retreats in beautiful locations around the world.

*Where can the readers find you?*

**Maria Koropecky:** Readers can find me online at ammolitewellnesscoaching.com. Go there to find out more about who I am, what it is that I do, and how exactly I can help you. I am also on LinkedIn as Maria Koropecky, although I'm not on any other social media sites. Wherever you go to find out more about me and my work, if anything interests you, you can schedule time with me over at

https://go.oncehub.com/MariaKoropeckysIntervi ewBookingLink.

# About Maria Koropecky

Maria Koropecky provides varied services, but one thing that unites them is that they all spring from a deep desire to help the imaginative people she meets. An introvert who has in the past struggled to come out of her shell and unleash her creativity, she uses the world around her to inspire confidence – not just in her clients, but in her own self, too.

Working out of British Columbia in Canada, she draws on the power of crystals and gemstones to help people stand in their power and go after what they want. She has alsodeveloped a unique approach to wellness coaching that she calls Crystal Mapping. The crystal maps she creates with her clients help them feel more connected to the earth and their feelings. In grounding them, Maria guides her clients to understand where they are at in their lives and to see with clarity exactly where they would like to go next.

The qualifications she has earned throughout her life inform the work she does, always. These range from the BA English Literature degree she graduated with when she was younger to the certifications in Life Coaching, Mentoring, and Crystal Reading that she has received in more recent years.

**WEBSITE**
AmmoliteWellnessCoaching.com/

**EMAIL**
maria@ammolitewellnesscoaching.com

www.ingramcontent.com/pod-product-compliance
Lightning Source LLC
Chambersburg PA
CBHW071110210326
41519CB00020B/6250